TRAVEL TO...
HISTORICALLY BLACK
COLLEGES AND UNIVERSITIES

J.P. Miller

Rourke.

BEFORE AND DURING READING ACTIVITIES

Before Reading: *Building Background Knowledge and Vocabulary*

Building background knowledge can help children process new information and build upon what they already know. Before reading a book, it is important to tap into what children already know about the topic. This will help them develop their vocabulary and increase their reading comprehension.

Questions and Activities to Build Background Knowledge:

1. Look at the front cover of the book and read the title. What do you think this book will be about?

2. What do you already know about this topic?

3. Take a book walk and skim the pages. Look at the table of contents, photographs, captions, and bold words. Did these text features give you any information or predictions about what you will read in this book?

Vocabulary: *Vocabulary Is Key to Reading Comprehension*

Use the following directions to prompt a conversation about each word:

- Read the vocabulary words.
- What comes to mind when you see each word?
- What do you think each word means?

Vocabulary Words:
- activists
- alumni
- bachelor's degrees
- boycott
- integrate
- master's degree
- philanthropist
- racial slurs
- scholarship
- segregation
- sit-in
- underrepresented communities

During Reading: *Reading for Meaning and Understanding*

To achieve deep comprehension of a book, children are encouraged to use close reading strategies. During reading, it is important to have children stop and make connections. These connections result in deeper analysis and understanding of a book.

 ### Close Reading a Text

During reading, have children stop and talk about the following:

- Any confusing parts
- Any unknown words
- Text to text, text to self, text to world connections
- The main idea in each chapter or heading

Encourage children to use context clues to determine the meaning of any unknown words. These strategies will help children learn to analyze the text more thoroughly as they read.

When you are finished reading this book, turn to page 45 for **Text-Dependent Questions** and an **Extension Activity**.

TABLE of CONTENTS

HISTORICALLY BLACK
COLLEGES AND UNIVERSITIES

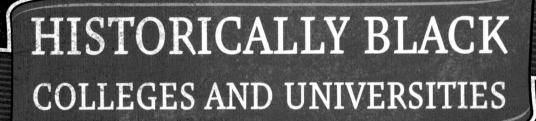

African Americans have always had a desire to learn. But laws of oppression were established with strict punishments that prohibited enslaved Black people from learning. Many of them risked their lives to pursue knowledge.

During the Civil Rights Movement, education was at the forefront of the battle cry for equality. Old laws were replaced by new ones. Black students were finally able to attend school—but not with White students.

So, Black-only primary and secondary schools popped up across America. But Black people yearned for more. Their sights were set on college.

Segregation's response to higher-level education for African Americans was Historically Black Colleges and Universities (HBCUs). HBCUs were excellent options for education then and they remain excellent options today. Come! Let's travel to … America's HBCUs!

HBCUs—IN THE BEGINNING

CHEYNEY UNIVERSITY
OF PENNSYLVANIA

The year was 1837. Martin Van Buren was to become the 8th president of the United States. The nation was divided about slavery, but something monumental happened in the state of Pennsylvania. Richard Humphreys, a **philanthropist**, willed one tenth of his estate to build a school for people of African descent.

The African Institute was the first school of higher education for African Americans in the country. Its mission was to teach students trades in agriculture and mechanics.

The school has undergone several name and location changes over the years. Now known as Cheyney University of Pennsylvania, it offers over 30 **bachelor's degrees** and a variety of master's programs.

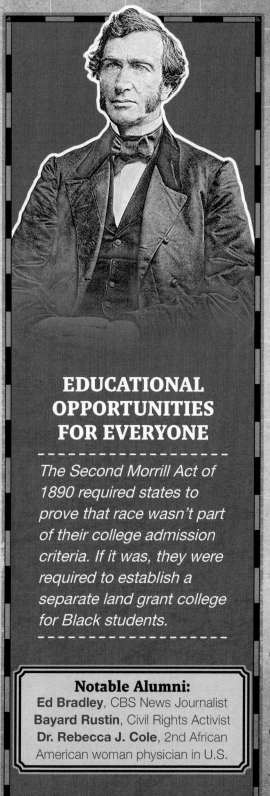

EDUCATIONAL OPPORTUNITIES FOR EVERYONE

The Second Morrill Act of 1890 required states to prove that race wasn't part of their college admission criteria. If it was, they were required to establish a separate land grant college for Black students.

Notable Alumni:
Ed Bradley, CBS News Journalist
Bayard Rustin, Civil Rights Activist
Dr. Rebecca J. Cole, 2nd African American woman physician in U.S.

SHAW UNIVERSITY

Less than a mile from the state capitol in Raleigh, North Carolina, sits Shaw University. It was one of the first HBCUs established in the South. Shaw University opened in 1865 when former Union Chaplin Henry Martin Tupper and his wife, Sarah, taught reading, writing, and Bible lessons to formerly enslaved people in their hotel room.

Classes grew larger. In 1866, the Tuppers, students, and friends built a new facility and named it the Raleigh Theological Institute.

Over the years, the campus grew and the school was renamed after Elijah Shaw, who funded its new construction. Today, Shaw covers over 24 acres and is one of the country's leading theological schools for Baptist ministers.

SHAW UNIVERS
FOUNDED 1865

LIMITLESS POSSIBILITIES

There are over 100 public and private HBCUs in the United States, including three that are gender specific. Collectively they offer 83 associate, 83 bachelor's, 27 doctoral, and 52 **master's degree** *programs.*

Notable Alumni:
Shirley Caesar, Grammy Award-Winning Gospel Singer
James "Bonecrusher" Smith, Heavyweight Boxing Champion

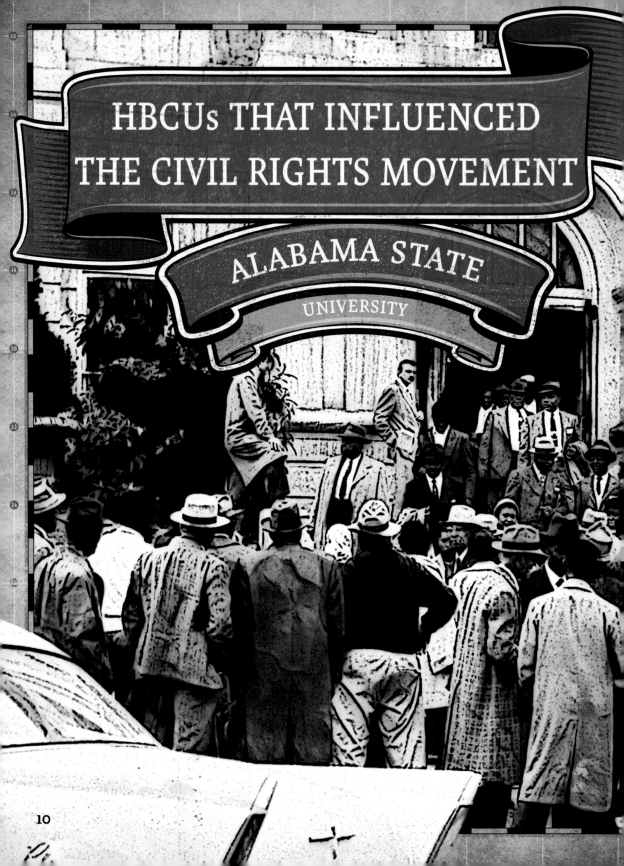

HBCUs THAT INFLUENCED THE CIVIL RIGHTS MOVEMENT

ALABAMA STATE

UNIVERSITY

Alabama State University was founded in Montgomery, Alabama, in 1867. It was one of the first state-supported HBCUs in the nation. Its faculty and students played a large role in the Civil Rights Movement.

On December 1, 1955, in Montgomery, Rosa Parks was arrested for not giving up her bus seat to a White rider. Black people in Montgomery were angry. It was time for action.

That night, Alabama State University professor Jo Ann Robinson rallied her students. She printed thousands of flyers announcing a one-day bus **boycott**. Students went door-to-door handing them out. This one-day boycott developed into a 381-day bus boycott that crippled the city financially. It spurred bus boycotts in other cities too.

Notable Alumni:
Rickey Smiley, Comedian/Actor
The Honorable Delores J. Thomas,
Former NY State
Supreme Court Justice

NORTH CAROLINA A&T
UNIVERSITY

F. W. WOOLV

On February 1, 1960, David Richmond, Franklin McCain, Ezell Blair Jr., and Joe McNeil etched their names in history. The North Carolina A&T students staged a **sit-in** at the food counter of the Greensboro Woolworth Department Store. They wanted to end the store's **segregation** policy.

Racial slurs were spewed at them. Punches were thrown at them. Police officers paced behind them, but the teens were not arrested. By staying calm and not fighting back, they set an example to other students of how to protest segregation peacefully. This was the beginning of sit-ins by HBCU students across the nation.

XAVIER UNIVERSITY
OF LOUISIANA

Notable Alumni:
Bryant Terry,
Chef/Food Justice Activist/Author
Dr. Regina Benjamin,
18th U.S. Surgeon General

By 1961, segregation on public buses had been ruled unconstitutional. However, southern states continued the practice. To challenge this, civil rights **activists** rode buses and tried to enter "White-only" areas in bus terminals. These activists, many of whom were HBCU students, were called Freedom Riders.

On May 15, 1961, an angry mob attacked the Freedom Riders in New Orleans, Louisiana, and destroyed their bus. They were stranded. Hotels refused them service.

Xavier University of Louisiana, the country's only Catholic HBCU, stepped in to help. Dr. Norman C. Francis, the university's president, secretly permitted the Freedom Riders to stay on campus for a week. Out of fear of retaliation, the public wasn't told they were staying there.

Freedom Riders

MOREHOUSE COLLEGE

At 11:00 a.m. on March 15, 1960, eleven sit-ins to protest segregation took place across Atlanta, Georgia. They were planned and organized by Morehouse College students Lonnie King, Charles Black, the Student Nonviolence Movement (SNM), and others. The SNM included all six Atlanta University Center HBCUs, making it one of the most collaborative protest efforts involving students.

The protest lasted a year! It targeted Rich's Department Store and other local businesses. It even affected the mayoral election that year.

Founded in 1867, Morehouse College is one of only a few gender-specific HBCUs. The all-male school was the training ground for many civil rights giants, including Dr. Martin Luther King, Jr.

MAKING A DIFFERENCE

- - - - - - - - - - - - - - - - - - - -

Students of HBCUs were integral in the success of the Civil Rights Movement. During sit-ins, marches, boycotts, Freedom Rides, and more, many were beaten and jailed, but they got right back up. Many campuses have monuments to honor their commitment and bravery.

- - - - - - - - - - - - - - - - - - - -

Notable Alumni:
Dr. Martin Luther King, **Jr**.,
Civil Rights Leader
Samuel L. Jackson, Actor

MEHARRY MEDICAL
COLLEGE

Students stand anxiously before their professors. On cue, a white medical jacket is draped on each one of them. This is their White Coat Ceremony, a rite of passage that symbolizes the transition from student to medical professional.

Since 1876, Meharry Medical College in Nashville, Tennessee, has sent several thousand doctors, dentists, and other medical professionals into the world. Donning their maroon-embroidered white coats, graduates understand the legacy that comes with wearing the Meharry name.

Meharry was the first medical college for Black people in the South. Its graduates are committed to serving **underrepresented communities**. Three out of every four Meharrians return to urban or rural communities to work after they graduate.

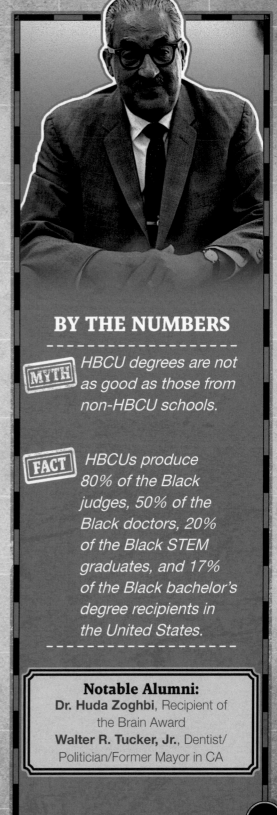

BY THE NUMBERS

MYTH
HBCU degrees are not as good as those from non-HBCU schools.

FACT
HBCUs produce 80% of the Black judges, 50% of the Black doctors, 20% of the Black STEM graduates, and 17% of the Black bachelor's degree recipients in the United States.

Notable Alumni:
Dr. Huda Zoghbi, Recipient of the Brain Award
Walter R. Tucker, Jr., Dentist/Politician/Former Mayor in CA

HOWARD UNIVERSITY

Howard University is one of the most competitive HBCUs in the country. With the nation's capital as its backdrop, it has been dubbed "The Mecca." Since 1867 when the school was founded, the brightest, most gifted students have competed for a spot here.

Howard University is best known for its STEM Education—more specifically, the Karsh STEM Scholar Program. The school searches for high school prodigies interested in earning a PhD in a STEM field. Then they help them fulfill their dream. The **scholarship** program pays for students' tuition, room and board, books, and overseas studies. The school and its programs support its motto, "Veritas et Utilitas – Truth and Service."

Notable Alumni:

Chadwick Boseman,
Actor/Playwright
Kamala Harris, Vice President
of the United States

MORGAN STATE
UNIVERSITY

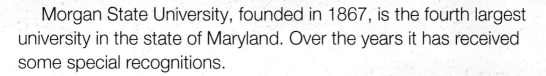

Morgan State University, founded in 1867, is the fourth largest university in the state of Maryland. Over the years it has received some special recognitions.

First, in 2016, it was designated as a National Treasure by the National Trust for Historic Preservation. This will help preserve the history of some of the school's oldest buildings.

Secondly, in 2017, the governor designated Morgan State as the state's preeminent public urban research university. It was deemed a level R2 research school, and it is on track to become an R1 research doctoral university. This would be a first for an HBCU. Only schools that do a very high level of research receive this distinction.

Notable Alumni:
April Ryan, Political Journalist
David E. Talbert, NAACP
Award-Winning Playwright/
Filmmaker/Author

Florida A&M (FAMU) has the number one-ranked law school of all HBCUs, but it didn't happen easily or overnight. It was decades in the making.

After five Black students were denied access into segregated University of Florida, FAMU's School of Law was formed in 1949. But, when Black students were allowed to **integrate** segregated schools in 1966, FAMU was told it had to stop admitting students into its law school. It was being shut down.

For the next 30 years, the university fought to have its law school reopened. No one worked harder for this than Frederick Humphries, FAMU president. On June 14, 2000, he succeeded, and the Florida A&M School of Law was reestablished.

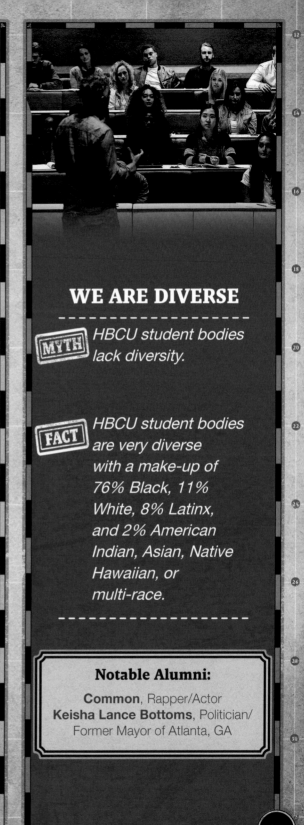

WE ARE DIVERSE

MYTH HBCU student bodies lack diversity.

FACT HBCU student bodies are very diverse with a make-up of 76% Black, 11% White, 8% Latinx, and 2% American Indian, Asian, Native Hawaiian, or multi-race.

Notable Alumni:

Common, Rapper/Actor
Keisha Lance Bottoms, Politician/ Former Mayor of Atlanta, GA

HBCUs—IMPRESSIVE ATHLETICS

JACKSON STATE
UNIVERSITY

Mississippi Veterans Memorial Stadium is packed. Over 60,000 Jackson State University students, **alumni**, and fans have donned their game-day blue and white. The Sonic Boom Marching Band energizes the crowd.

In 2020, NFL and MLB standout Deion "Primetime" Sanders became JSU's new head football coach, where he would stay for three seasons. He was the first NFL Football Hall of Famer to coach an HBCU football team. In his first year at JSU, he led the JSU Tigers to an 11-game winning season. For the first time since 2007, they also won the SWAC Championship.

HBCU football goes way back. The first football game between HBCUs was in 1892 between Livingstone College and Johnson C. Smith University.

HBCU CONFERENCES

The most popular athletic conferences for HBCUs are the Southwestern Athletic Conference (SWAC), the Mid-Eastern Athletic Conference (MEAC), the Central Intercollegiate Athletic Association (CIAA), and the Southern Intercollegiate Athletic Conference (SIAC).

Notable Alumni:

Vivian Brown,
Weather Channel Meteorologist
Walter Payton, Former
Chicago Bears Running Back

FISK UNIVERSITY

Brown girls leap across mats. They mount uneven bars and execute half levers on the balance beam. These girls are members of the Fisk University Bulldogs gymnastics team. In 2022, the university added gymnastics to their roster of sports. It was the first time gymnastics had ever been offered at an HBCU.

For 5-star recruit Morgan Price, this was a dream come true. She had always wanted to compete in gymnastics at an HBCU. So she de-committed from Arkansas University and committed to Fisk University in Nashville.

Founded in 1866, Fisk University is the oldest school of higher learning in Tennessee.

Notable Alumni:
John Lewis, Politician/Activist
Nikki Giovanni, Poet/Activist

TEXAS SOUTHERN
UNIVERSITY

Every spring, the best college basketball teams in the nation meet for the National Collegiate Athletics Association (NCAA) Men's Basketball Tournament. March Madness showcases the teams battling it out to be #1.

The Texas Southern Tigers have played in the tournament ten times. Their big 2021 victory over Mount St. Mary's etched the 95-year-old institution in college basketball history and brought thousands of dollars to the school. They were one of the first HBCUs to ever win a game during March Madness. Then, in 2022, they defeated Texas A&M-Corpus Christi in the First Four games.

Television coverage featuring HBCUs has increased the interest of high school athletes in attending an HBCU for athletics. In 2021, Shaquir O'Neal, youngest son of NBA's Shaquille O'Neal, committed to play basketball at Texas Southern.

THEY'LL KNOW YOUR NAME

 HBCUs don't have good sports programs.

 HBCU athletes have gone on to play in the NFL, NBA, MLB, and compete in the Olympics. The Tennessee State University men's basketball team was a national champion three years in a row—from 1957-1959.

Notable Alumni:

Barbara Jordan,
Politician/Lawyer/Educator
Michael Strahan,
Journalist/Former NFL Player

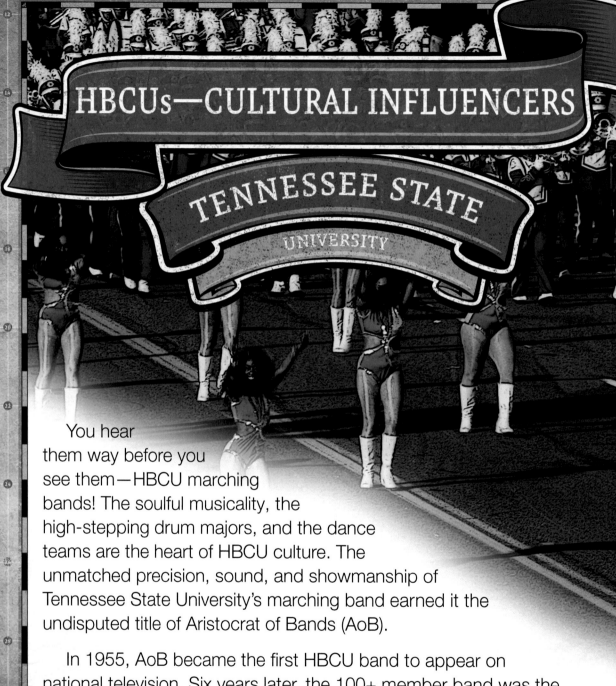

HBCUs—CULTURAL INFLUENCERS

TENNESSEE STATE UNIVERSITY

You hear them way before you see them—HBCU marching bands! The soulful musicality, the high-stepping drum majors, and the dance teams are the heart of HBCU culture. The unmatched precision, sound, and showmanship of Tennessee State University's marching band earned it the undisputed title of Aristocrat of Bands (AoB).

In 1955, AoB became the first HBCU band to appear on national television. Six years later, the 100+ member band was the first HBCU to perform at a presidential inauguration. In 2022, AoB released their first album—The Urban Hymnal. The album won a Grammy Award, making the AoB the first marching band to ever win a Grammy.

GET ON UP!

HBCU marching bands can get any crowd to their feet with their energetic performances. Their distinctive high-stepping style of marching originated in the 1940s. It is a combination of military style marching and minstrel shows. Each year, HBCU bands compete for bragging rights in the Honda Battle of the Bands.

Notable Alumni:

Robert Covington, NBA player
Oprah Winfrey, Talk Show Host/
Movie Producer/Philanthropist

FISK UNIVERSITY

In addition to their sports, Fisk University is also known for its music. When the Fisk Jubilee Singers take the stage, their tenor, soprano, and alto voices blend like the sound of angels. It is because of this group that Nashville, Tennessee, is called "Music City."

The Fisk Jubilee Singers was formed in 1871 as a fundraiser to help the school stay afloat. They did that and more. The group raised all the money for the construction of Jubilee Hall and for most of the land the campus sits on today.

The Fisk Jubilee Singers introduced African American spirituals, also known as Negro spirituals, or "slave songs," to the world. The legacy of these songs remains strong in Black culture. The group has received the National Medal of Art, a Dove Award, and has been nominated for a Grammy.

Jubilee Singers

MUSIC CITY, USA

Many people think that Nashville is called "Music City" because of country music. But it's believed that the nickname comes from a compliment given by Queen Victoria following a Fisk Jubilee Singers concert in Great Britain.

Notable Alumni:

Booker T. Washington, Influential Speaker and Educator
Kym Whitley, Actress/Comedian

BENEDICT COLLEGE

Every drumbeat, guitar strum, and melody made by the Benedict College Gospel Choir is for the glory of God. Over the years the choir has grown from 20 members to over 160 members, but its purpose has stayed the same—to spread the gospel throughout the world.

Gospel choirs hold a sacred place in HBCU culture. The Benedict College Gospel Choir has performed around the world and won several choir competitions along the way. Some call them "the best gospel choir in the galaxy."

Benedict College is in Columbia, South Carolina. It was founded in 1870 by the American Baptist Home Mission Society.

Notable Alumni:

Septima Poinsette Clark,
Educator/"Queen Mother of the
Civil Rights Movement"
Craig A. Williams, President of the
Jordan Brand for Nike

HBCUs WITH THE MOST

INTERESTING TRIVIA

WILBERFORCE

UNIVERSITY

The Tawawa House in Wilberforce, Ohio, was once a place of refuge for Freedom Seekers on the Underground Railroad. In 1856, the 300-room house became a school.

The African Methodist Episcopal Church founded Wilberforce College, making it the first private HBCU founded by African Americans. Wilberforce is one of 37 private HBCUs that partners with the United Negro College Fund and benefits from their donations.

In 1863, Bishop Daniel Payne became its president. He was the first president of African descent to lead an American institution of higher learning. In 1965, the school was renamed Wilberforce University.

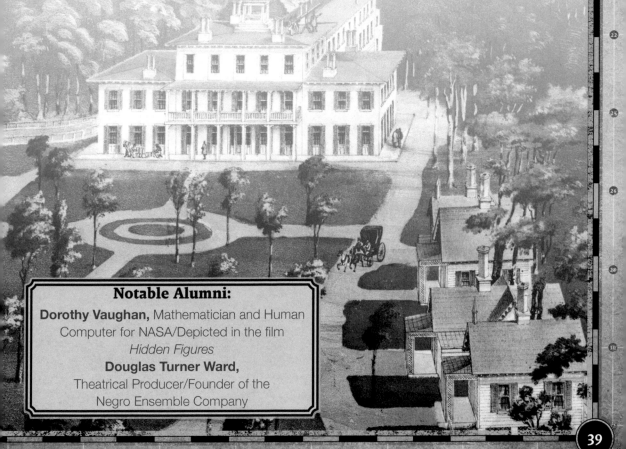

Notable Alumni:

Dorothy Vaughan, Mathematician and Human Computer for NASA/Depicted in the film *Hidden Figures*

Douglas Turner Ward, Theatrical Producer/Founder of the Negro Ensemble Company

BETHUNE-COOKMAN
UNIVERSITY

INFLUENTIAL WOMEN

The other three Black women who founded an HBCU are:

*Elizabeth Evelyn Wright, Voorhees College – Denmark, SC (1897)

*Annie M. Turnbo Pope Malone, Poro College – St. Louis, MO (1917)

*Dr. Violet Temple Lewis, Lewis College of Business - Indianapolis, IN (1928)

Notable Alumni:

Marjorie Joyner, Inventor/ Permanent Wave Machine
John Chaney, Former Men's Basketball Coach at Temple University

The larger-than-life statue of Dr. Mary McCleod Bethune stands watch over Bethune-Cookman University in Daytona Beach, Florida. She is one of four African American women to have founded an HBCU. With only $1.50, she started the Daytona Literary and Industrial Training School for Negro Girls in 1904. Her first class included five little girls and her son, Albert.

Over the years, the school has had several name changes. In 1923, Dr. Bethune merged her school with the Cookman Institute in Jacksonville, Florida. It became Daytona-Cookman Collegiate Institute. In 1931, the school's name changed again. This time it bore her name—Bethune-Cookman. It became a university in 2007.

Historically Black Colleges and Universities were created when Black students could not attend White schools. Nearly 200 years later, they are hidden gems in America's educational system. Students of all races are empowered by the pride, culture, and history of HBCUs. There's an expectation from alumni, faculty, and students that this great legacy will continue.

HIGH STANDARDS

- - - - - - - - - - - - - - - - - - -

MYTH HBCUs are easy to get into and will accept anyone.

FACT HBCU's admissions policies encourage inclusivity, but their academic standards are demanding. They prepare students for real-world experiences.

- - - - - - - - - - - - - - - - - - -

COMPLETE LIST OF ALL HBCUs

Alabama A&M University (1875)

Alabama State University (1867)

Albany State University (1903)

Alcorn State University (1871)

Allen University (1870)

American Baptist College (1924)

University of Arkansas-Pine Bluff (1873)

Arkansas Baptist College (1884)

Barba-Scotia College (1867)

Benedict College (1870)

Bennett College (1873)

Bethune-Cookman University (1904)

Bishop State Community College (1927)

Bluefield State College (1895)

Bowie State University (1865)

Central State University (1837)

Charles Drew University of Medicine and Science (1966)

Cheyney University of Pennsylvania (1837)

Claflin University (1869)

Clark Atlanta University (1865)

Clinton College (1894)

Coahoma Community College (1924)

Coppin State University (1900)

Delaware State University (1891)

Denmark Technical College (1947)

Dillard University (1869)

University of the District of Columbia (1851)

Edward Waters University (1866)

Elizabeth City State University (1891)

Fayetteville State University (1867)

Fisk University (1866)

Florida A&M University (1887)

Florida Memorial University (1879)

Fort Valley State University (1895)

Gadsden State Community College (1925)

Grambling State University (1901)

Hampton University (1868)

Harris-Stowe State University (1857)

Hinds Community College at Utica (1917)

Howard University (1867)

Hutson-Tillotson University (1875)

Interdenominational Theological Center (1958)

J.F. Drake State Technical College (1961)

Jackson State University (1877)

Jarvis Christian College (1912)

Johnson C. Smith University (1867)

Kentucky State University (1886)

Knoxville College (1875)

Lane College (1882)

Langston University (1897)

Lawson State Community College (1949)

LeMoyne-Owen College (1871)

Lincoln University (1854)

Lincoln University of Missouri (1866)

Livingstone College (1879)

University of Maryland Eastern Shore (1886)

Meharry Medical College (1876)

Miles College (1898)

Mississippi Valley State University (1950)

Morehouse College (1867)

Morgan State University (1867)

Morris Brown College (1881)

Morris College (1908)

Norfolk State University (1935)

North Carolina A&T University (1891)

North Carolina Central University (1910)

Oakwood University (1896)

Paine College (1882)

Paul Quinn College (1872)

Payne Theological Seminary (1894)

Philander Smith College (1877)

Prairie View A&M University (1876)

Rust College (1866)

Savannah State University (1890)

Selma University (1878)

Shaw University (1865)

Shorter College (1886)

Shelton State Community College (1952)

Simmons College (1899)

South Carolina State University (1896)

Southern University at New Orleans (1959)

Southern University Law School (1946)

Southern University (1880)

Southwestern Christian College (1948)

Spelman College (1881)

St. Augustine's University (1867)

St. Philip's College (1898)

Stillman College (1876)

Talladega College (1867)

Tennessee State University (1912)

Texas College (1894)

Texas Southern University (1927)

Tougaloo College (1869)

Trenholm State Community College (1947)

Tuskegee University (1881)

University of the Virgin Islands (1962)

Virginia State University (1882)

Virginia Union University (1865)

Virginia University of Lynchburg (1886)

Voorhees College (1897)

West Virginia State University (1891)

Wilberforce University (1856)

Wiley College (1873)

Winston-Salem State University (1892)

Xavier University of Louisiana (1915)

GLOSSARY

activist (AK-tuh-vist): a person who believes in and fights for equal rights for all people

alumni (uh-LUM-nye): people who attended or graduated from a college or university

bachelor's degrees (BACH-uh-lurs di-GREEZ): diplomas given when people graduate from a college or university

boycott (BOI-kaht): to refuse to do business with someone as a protest

integrate (IN-ti-grate): to bring groups together

master's degree (MAS-turs di-GREE): a diploma students earn when they complete studies beyond a bachelor's degree

philanthropist (fuh-LAN-thruh-pist): a person who gives time or money to help causes or charities

racial slurs (RAY-shuhl slurs): insults based on someone's race

scholarship (SKAH-lur-ship): money given to pay for someone's college or course of study

segregation (seg-ri-GAY-shuhn): the separation or isolation of a race, class, or ethnic group

sit-in (sit-in): an act of sitting in seats or on the floor as a means of an organized protest

underrepresented communities (UHN-dur-rep-ri-zent-ed kuh-MYO-ni-tees): an area or group of people poorly represented within a majority population

INDEX

TEXT-DEPENDENT QUESTIONS

1. What was the importance of the Second Morrill Act of 1890?

2. Which HBCU is designated a National Treasure?

3. Why were the Fisk Jubilee Singers formed?

4. What did the students of North Carolina A&T do that influenced the Civil Rights Movement?

5. Which HBCU was the first to be owned and operated by African Americans?

EXTENSION ACTIVITY

There are over 100 HBCUs in 19 states. Take a virtual tour of as many of them as you can. Go to the schools' official websites and look them up on YouTube. Do any suit your interests or academic goals? If possible, plan a road trip with your family to explore a few of your top choices. Share the information you learn with friends and family.

BIBLIOGRAPHY

"Voices of the Civil Rights Movement: The Student Nonviolence Movement." *YouTube*, uploaded by Comcast NBC, 12 August 2021. https://www.youtube.com/channel/UCDoz3ZyvhpqGhTj4L7V0O3g.

"Texas Southern vs. Texas A&M – First Four NCAA Tournament…" *YouTube*, uploaded by ESPN, 15 March 2022, https://www.youtube.com/watch?v=hR8vvDtWaj8

"History of Florida A&M University College of Law." *YouTube*, uploaded by FAMU Law, 2 August 2018, https://www.youtube.com/watch?v=eJ3lvs-LKjU.

Garriga, Geovann Ariel, et. al. "Freedom Riders at Xavier University." *New Orleans Historical.* 12 September 2022. https://neworleanshistorical.org/items/show/1493.

Grove, Rashaad, "These Former Pro Athletes are Coaches at HBCUs." *Ebony*. 21 October 2021, https://www.ebony.com/these-former-pro-athletes-are-coaches-at-hbcus/.

Hachette, Ford. "NC A&T Marks 61 Years Since the Sit-In that Fueled the Civil Rights Movement." WXII 12 (Greensboro, NC). 1 February 2021, https://www.wxii12.com/article/ncat-four-61anniversary/35385549.

"5 Colleges that were Started by or Named After Black Women." *Historically Black Since*, 19 August 2020, http://news.hbcusince.com/2020/08/5-colleges-that-were-started-by-or-named-after-black-women/.

"Patents Assigned to Morgan State University." *Justia Patents*, 2022, https://patents.justia.com/assignee/morgan-state-university.

Mobley-Martinez, T.D. "Benedicts Gospel Singers Uplift Spirits with Music," The State (Columbia, SC).

"HBCUs See Soring Applications." *YouTube*, uploaded by Kenneth Moten, ABC News. 7 June 2021, https://www.youtube.com/watch?v=H-ApB1_IJrE.

BIBLIOGRAPHY

"Tell Them We Are Rising: The History of HBCUs in America," PBS, Independent Lens. *YouTube*, uploaded by Stanley Nelson and Marco Williams, 31 January 2019, https://www.youtube.com/watch?v=FTbtYCy3KeM.

"Shaquir O'Neal is Committed!..." *YouTube*, uploaded by Overtime, 22 July 21. https://www.youtube.com/watch?v=QA4D1akf6sI.

Peck, Timothy. "What is Howard University Known For?" *College Vine Blog*. https://blog.collegevine.com/what-is-howard-university-known-for.

"Shaw Rising." *YouTube*, uploaded by Shaw University, 17 April 2020. https://www.youtube.com/watch?v=Pe3ckZPy5M8.

Smith, Denise A. "The Facts on HBCUs: Top 10 Facts about Historically Black Colleges and Universities." *The Century Foundation*. 9 September 2022. https://tcf.org/content/commentary/the-facts-on-hbcus-top-10-facts-about-historically-black-colleges-and-universities/.

Stephenson, Jemma. "'From These Couches': How Alabama State University Has a Long History with Civil Rights." *The Montgomery Advertiser*. 9 February 2022 (Updated 11 Feb 2022). https://www.montgomeryadvertiser.com/story/news/2022/02/10/alabama-state-universitys-history-intertwined-civil-rights/6663185001/.

"Fisk University First Ever Women's Gymnastics Practice Goes Viral." *YouTube*, uploaded by USA Today, 17 August 22. https://www.youtube.com/watch?v=ysmX65ikwEg.

"HBCUs Seeing Resurgence of Interest, Applications." *YouTube*, uploaded by WCNC News (Charlotte, NC), 1 February 2021. https://www.youtube.com/watch?v=XUy3uB8Otvg.

"Coppell Gymnast Decommits from SEC School for Spot on First HBCU Gymnastics Team." *YouTube*, uploaded by WFAA, 5 July 2022. https://www.youtube.com/watch?v=kSbjLHD1s_c.

As a high school standout in track and field, J.P. Miller hoped to follow in the footsteps of the great Olympic runner Wilma Rudolph. Though she did not make the famous Tigerbelle Track Team, J.P. is a proud graduate of Tennessee State University. As a writer, J.P. enjoys bringing people and events in Black history to life for young readers.

www.rourkebooks.com

PHOTO CREDITS ©: Cover: Andrey_Kuzmin/ Shutterstock.com; Cover: Jennifer_Sharp/ Getty Images; Cover: Marco Rubino/ Shutterstock.com; Cover: Diego Grandi/ Shutterstock.com; Cover: michaeljung/ Getty Images; Cover: Oakley/ Shutterstock.com; Page 1: Prostock-studio/ Shutterstock.com; Page 4-5: National Archives, Records of the National Park Service; Page 6-7: ASSOCIATED PRESS; Page 7: Library of Congress Prints and Photographs Division. Brady-Handy Photograph Collection; Page 8-9: Wileydoc/ Shutterstock.com; Page 9: Prostock-studio/ Shutterstock.com; Page 10-11: Everett Collection/ Newscom; Page 11: GG Vintage Images/Newscom; Page 12-13: Bob Karp/ ZUMAPRESS/ Newscom; Page 14-15: University of College/ Shutterstock.com; Page 15: Underwood Archives/ UIG/ Newscom; Page16-17: ASSOCIATED PRESS; Page 17: Bob Karp/ ZUMAPRESS/ Newscom; Page 18-19: FatCamera/ Getty Images; Page 19: National Archives/ TNS/ Newscom; Page 20-21: gorodenkoff/ Getty Images; Page 22-23: Amy Davis/ TNS/ Newscom; Page 24-25: DPST/ Newscom; Page 25: monkeybusinessimages/ Getty Images; Page 26: Michael Wade/ Icon Sportswire CGW/ Newscom; Page 26-27: April Visuals/ Shutterstock.com; Page 27: Romeo Guzman/ Cal Sport Media/ Newscom; Page 28-29: Amy Sanderson/ ZUMAPRESS/ Newscom; Page 30-31: Thurman James/ Cal Sport Media/ Newscom; Page 31: ASSOCIATED PRESS; PAGE 32-33: Joe Sohm/ Universal Images Group/ Newscom; Page 33: Brian Cahn/ ZUMApress/ Newscom; Page 34: CHUCK LIDDY/ MCT/ Newscom; Page 34-35: Christopher L. Smith/ agefotostock/ Newscom; Page 35: Joseph Sohm/ Shutterstock.com; Page 36-37: Wirestock/ Getty Images; Page 38-39: World History Archive/ Newscom; Page 40: null/ Newscom; Page 41: Carl Van Vechten/ Library of Congress/ Wikimedia Commons; Page 41: Cheriss May/ ZUMA Press/ Newscom; Page various: LoudRedCreative/ Getty Images; Page various: Anna Timoshenko/ Shutterstock.com; Page various: Miodrag Kitanovic/ Getty Images; Page various: Andrey_Kuzmin/ Shutterstock.com

Library of Congress PCN Data

Historically Black Colleges and Universities / J.P. Miller

(Travel to...)

ISBN 978-1-73165-730-5 (hard cover)

ISBN 978-1-73165-717-6 (soft cover)

ISBN 978-1-73165-743-5 (e-book)

ISBN 978-1-73165-756-5 (e-pub)

Library of Congress Control Number: 2023941365

Rourke Educational Media

Printed in the United States of America

02-1512411937

Edited by: **Catherine Malaski**

Cover and interior design/illustration by: **Max Porter**